Seeing Life Along the Glass

Greg Kilberger

Copyright © 2013 Greg Kilberger
Cover and interior art by Teresa McCarthy

All rights reserved.

ISBN-10:0615741207
ISBN-13:9780615741208

DEDICATION

To Diane.
Without you, this would never have been possible. With love, respect, and hope. Always.

Stephanie, thank you for your invaluable encouragement.

Teresa, for your art and your excitement.

Bert, thanks for being there.

And thank you Mom.

CONTENTS

Preface	i
Looking Through	1
Reflections	26
The Edge	70

PREFACE

To me, poetry is emotion. You can express emotion through the writing of poetry. You can convey emotion to others through the reading or reciting of poetry. You can discover and feel emotion by reading or listening to poetry. What is beautiful about this process is that these emotions do not have to be the same for the creator as they are for the recipient. Poetry is, often times, open to interpretation. This is why poetry can be enjoyed by so many people for years and years. Otherwise, only a scant few could derive any meaning from it.

Contained in this book are poems that have leapt from my brain over the years. Many are the result of situations or people that I have experienced, but not all. Some are from nothing more than my fancy. I hope that these works of poetry find emotion in you. Anger, sorrow or joy, all are welcome. Come, step inside.

<blockquote>
I am a Poet
I am a Writer
I am an Actor
I am a Father
All else is subject to change
</blockquote>

Author's note: At times, I have gone back and revisited a poem. Not an editing, but simply a new look at the work. This has resulted in a change of rhythm or even point of view. There are a few poems in here that are similar to another. I decided to include both versions because they created a different enough voice to be heard again.

Greg Kilberger

LOOKING THROUGH

-CHOICE-

Destiny leads you along by the nose
Fate lets you choose which direction you go
One gives you no choice, this is the way
The other gives bricks that still you must lay
A timeline, or a guideline; a trick or a treat
Either way you must choose a lifetime to greet
But Destiny, she already knows what you will decide
As Lady Fate gives you choices, not along for the ride
So I disallow Destiny, I choose my own way
And I thank Fate for granting me choices each day
For Fate, though often cruel, to me will be true
For it is through Miss Fate that I ever met you.

Greg Kilberger

-SONNET-

Love is the cruelest lover that I know
She hides from you when you wish for her touch.
She hurts you, leaves you 'fraid to let it show
Yet you want her back, it ne'er is enough.
Kisses you, and makes each caress a sting
Holds you close, and warms you for all the night.
Yet each morning, fear and worry bring
What if it's all wrong, what if it's all right.
Finally you can tame her, so you think
You settle in and make her all your own.
Feeling safe and sure, you stand upon the brink
'Til she dangles you o'er the fallen stone,
Below you see a new love growing near
Once again she has you, ensnared with fear.

-BUCKET-

Your heart is a bucket
In which you carry your love.
It is silly but it is true.
Slowly you fill it when you are young,
Even though sometimes it feels like it holds the ocean.
Sometimes it gets dropped, or kicked, and it all pours away.
Those days are rough with tears.
But it can be filled again, and it will be.
One day you will find your bucket full to the top, dripping, running over.
Glories to the full vessel, it will not burst.
But be mindful
For if you don't pay attention, as you meander through life's path,
You may slop and spill without notice
And when you once again look down, the bucket may have almost drained away.
And it evaporates.
Some simply drop the bucket and walk away, wondering, confused.
But remember, you need only return to the spring to make the levels rise.
Plunge your bucket deep into the water.
Draw it up full again, drink it's sweetness in.
Do not be afraid, do not run away, do not close the door.
Just remember to glance at your bucket.
And visit the well often.

Greg Kilberger

-MY FAIREST LADY-

I still remember the first day that I saw you.
Your long blonde hair in your eyes.
I chased after you, you thought it cute
To run from me, run like the wind.
Then you let me catch you, and what fun.
Oh, those nights in my bed we spent
Just lying there with the TV on.
You'd curl up next to me and kiss
The knuckles on my left hand.
I'd try to keep myself warm
With just your heat, my body curled up
Around yours like a question mark.
But now my body lies as an exclamation
All alone and loud.
You flew from me like a hummingbird
I look for you every day, in the park
On the street, in the yard.
People say I'll get over you,
That it's only puppy love… I don't know
I still remember the first day I saw you.

-RESOLVE-

Dig down deep, steel your resolve
Ignore what they tell you, ignore it all
They do not know, they only guess
Trying to put you with all the rest
Find your purpose, find your role
Only then can you reach your goal
Do not give in, do not relent
Until all of your energy's spent
Ever forward you shall go
That is how we live and grow

Greg Kilberger

-LET ME BE YOUR UMBRELLA-

When your days get cloudy
Or your nights fill with storms
And you feel all alone
Just come take my hand
And I will help you
Find your way home.
When life's problems
Fill up the air
And rains down upon you
You don't need to hide,
Just look for me,
I will see you through.
If it gets too cold
And a blizzard of worry
Threatens to overcome
Just walk beside me
And feel my warmth
The fears will then be gone.
Let me be your umbrella.

-AFIRE-

My heart is afire
    My desire in flames
        The yearning grows higher
            The pyre yet remains
I sit in the white hot light
    As night is kept at bay
        My soul soars in flight
            Right from that first day
You've broken my shell
    I dwelt in for so long
        Without you would be a hell
            Unwell as well as wrong
But now we are forever
    Together just as one
        No matter what or whether
            Until our lives are done

Greg Kilberger

-DIANE'S SONG (I WANT TO HOLD)-

It has been so long since I truly saw you
Like a forgotten song, you are familiar but new
Now that you are here, I have got to tell you
All the things that I want to do
I want to hold your hand
In mine
I want to taste your lips
Like wine
I want to tell the world
You're mine
I just want to hold your hand
Now when I see your eyes, I feel the twinkle inside
And when I hear your voice my heart it bursts open wide
Won't you sit with me and let me tell you with pride
All the things that I want to do
I want to hold your hand
In mine
I want to taste your lips
Like wine
I want to tell the world
You're mine
I just want to hold your hand
By now you should know that I'll always be true
And forevermore I will deeply love you
I just hope and pray that you can say it too
All the things that I want to do
I want to hold your hand
In mine
I want to taste your lips
Like wine
I want to tell the world
You're mine
I just want to hold your hand

-DIANE-

I have seen her dancing-
Oh the way she dances!
The moves so full of style
Soft and lilting like the wind.
The grace of the majestic swan
Upon a moonlit surface.
The beauty of a thousand maidens
Could not shine so bright.
The might of a thousand men
Would not be as strong.
And that is just her eyes.

Greg Kilberger

-LOOK INSIDE-

Just look inside
You will see
All the things
You could be
Own the world
Find your love
Even reach
The stars above
What you want
May be out there
But what you need
Is right in here
So when you go
Into each day
Be prepared
Come what may
Face your future
Eyes open wide
Leave your fears
Nowhere to hide
You will not
Fail or die
Find the strength
Just look inside

-BROKEN-

I am not broken I am bruised
Time will heal all my wounds
Tomorrow may the sun shine
And contentment become mine
Today my outlook may be bleak
But that does not make me weak
Stand up and persevere
Learn from the pain of each tear
I am not broken I am whole
Find my peace that is my goal
Every morning this I say
That is how I face each day

Greg Kilberger

-MARRIAGE-

We start out young but not for long
Days go by and time moves on.
Seasons change and fashions too
But I still see your love is true.

Through summers heat and winters frost
Your companionship is never lost.
Even if troubles rise or buildings fall
Your love will stand throughout it all.

These past ten years I've seen you grow
Together more and more it shows
That your love will stand the test of time
Together you will walk love's line.

I speak the truth as everyone knows
The warmth between you grows and grows
And I smile when I hear the harmony
As your souls sing out their melody.

-TRUE-

This verse has no fancy hidden meaning
Just simple lines and rhyme scheming
A solid voice and pleasant word
Without images trite or absurd
Its only purpose is to grant a view
Into my soul and tell you true
So now you know, I love you.

Greg Kilberger

-HEART IS A BUCKET-

Your heart is a bucket to carry your love,
Slowly you fill it when you are young,
Sometimes it feels like it holds an ocean.
Sometimes it gets dropped, kicked, it pours away.
But it can be filled again, and it will be.
One day your bucket will be full to the top,
Dripping, running over, it will not burst.

But be mindful

For you may slop and spill without notice.
And when you once again look down,
The bucket may have almost drained away.
Some drop the bucket and walk away,
But you need only return to the spring.
Plunge your bucket deep in.
Draw it up full again, drink its sweetness.
Do not be afraid, do not run away.
Just remember to glance at your bucket.
And visit the well often.

-CIRCLES DANCED-

Close to midnight it's getting dark
Everywhere but inside my heart
I see your glow, you feel my heat
With circles danced where fingers meet.

I fight desire because I must
But ere these memories fade to dust
I cling to them with all my might
No matter if it's wrong or right.

Life is not always a kind thing
It gives you joy, but with a sting
Yet deep within, I shall hold it dear
To feel your closeness ever near.

The hour is late upon our time
Yet my heart's poem still has rhyme
For I feel a passion once again
This ghost will stir within, never end.

Those circles danced, I still can feel
Your warming touch is still so real
I wish fingertips were bodies whole
And our dance would have no toll.

Greg Kilberger

-THE DEW-

The Dew seeks her at night.
Away from the sun's harsh glare.
He caresses her, the Grass,
And keeps her safe
              And wet.
All night long.
As he holds her close to his body,
She clings to him as if to life itself.
And yet, despite her desire,
She lets him come and go at his fancy,
For she knows he will return again
              With the night.

-LOVE-

Love is a word that is hard to define,
   for it is not one single thing.
Love brings joy and pain and confusion
   and even the desire to sing.
You can love food or your job, your parents
   and kids, even love a song.
And even if others do not agree with you
   that doesn't mean you're wrong.
For love is a personal thing,
   each of us chooses to what it is assigned.
And sometimes those choices make no sense,
   for love, you see, is blind.
It doesn't care if it fits your plan for life,
Love does not consultate.
Instead it forces you to embrace what it has
   put upon your plate.
And the loves of my life are what helps define me,
   a sum of that math.
Love adds and love multiplies
   and the product thereof shows me my path.
But sometimes love subtracts from you
   and sometimes it causes divides.
And when those divisions come to light,
   you're in for a hell of a ride.
And then you find that love can hurt
   and love can cause much pain.
And though you wish to make it disappear
   it will linger just the same.
There are many things in my life
   that I can honestly say that I love.
Food and movies and certain songs,
   and pondering the stars above.

Greg Kilberger

And though these may change
  as I go through life, some will wax or wane.
They will always be a part of me,
  my love for them will surely remain.
It is so very hard to define the word love,
  that is most certainly true.
But one thing that is not hard to say
  is that I will always love you.

-I NEED YOUR LOVIN'-

My life used to get me down
Always all dark and grey
I hoped someone would come along
But no one ever stayed

I need your lovin' you know it's true
I need your lovin' 'cause I love you

But ever since I met you
My world has turned around
Everything's going my way now
No sadness to be found

And I owe it all to you girl
This life I'm living now
Just give me your lovin'
Cause I need it, I need it, I need it now.

I need your lovin' you know it's true
I need your lovin' 'cause I love you

Although we're sometimes far apart
Many times I cant be there
You know I will always love you
You know I'll always care

I need your lovin' you know it's true
I need your lovin' 'cause I love you
I love you.

Greg Kilberger

-THIS ISN'T ABOUT ANYTHING-

This isn't about you and what you have done
This isn't about me and what I have said
This isn't about us, or what has went wrong
This isn't about anything so just let it be.

Why does everything I do have to have meaning?
why does every written word have to be re-read?
Why can't we just accept things as part of living?
Open our minds and souls and just live free?

Now can't I see this was never about him?
Now can't I feel more alive and less dead?
Now can't you see this was never about her?
It is only about the love between you and me.

-CAN'T DO A THING-

I hear my phone, it's your ring tone
And all I want to do is cry.
I should get your call, but I know it's all
About leaving and goodbye.
I know that you, never wanted to
Make me feel all this pain.
Yet I believe, that when you leave
I will never want to smile again.

You can't write a sad song when you're happy
You can't talk about joy when you're blue
You can't sing about love when you're lonely
And I can't do a thing without you.
No I can't do a thing without you.

It's getting late, but I hesitate
To take myself to sleep.
When I hit the bed, you fill my head
And I just lie there and weep.
So I'm sitting here, with one more beer
Waiting on the dawn.
Then I will face, one more day
Just to try to carry on.

You can't write a sad song when you're happy
You can't talk about joy when you're blue
You can't sing about love when you're lonely
And I can't do a thing without you.
No I can't do a thing without you.

Today you're coming by, and I know why
It's to get your stuff and leave.
Now when you show, gonna watch you go

Greg Kilberger

But in my heart I still believe,
That our love's not gone, I will carry on
And pray you will someday see,
You're my turtle dove, and you need my love
And you will come on back to me.

You can't write a sad song when you're happy
You can't talk about joy when you're blue
You can't sing about love when you're lonely
And I can't do a thing without you.
No I can't do a thing without you.

-WHYGTL?-

I wonder what to do?
    Should I even try?
        It's not like you really seem to want me to.
I know I won't forget
    The mistakes I've made
        For the greatest pain is the pain of regret.
I see your smile,
    And want it all my life
        But today it only seems to last a little while
I love you,
    And if you will let me
        I can make you feel that love again too.

What have you got to lose?

-THE CUTTING WIT OF RYKOLII RUFKYN-

Just take your ease and listen to my tale
And you shall hear young Rykolii prevail.
Tis not another fill'd with demon hordes,
Instead a simple lodge with room and board.
Young Ryk was greeted at the door by all.
Begged he was to tell his latest triumph,
And so he did, til one man said "harumph,
Your tales are false, they just gratify the bored.
I doubt you e'en know how to use that sword."
Young Ryk replied "Good Sir, what ails you so?
They are good-natured yarns, not blow for blow.
But argue if you must my verbal foe."
At this the man replied, "You snotty lad,
I'll be your foe," his sword now in his hand.
Rykolii is taken aback; amazed.
He drops his glass and quickly goes to waist.
Rapier and stiletto fly, all a blur,
And dance forward toward the angry cur.
Fearful now, the big lout swings at Ryk's head,
But Ryk's parry blow leaves him unarmed instead.
Now cut and slash and flash throughout the joint,
And the bully sees Rykolii's true point.
A belt hanging from the end of Ryk's steel,
The lout's pants a-fall; a breeze now he feels.
Unarmed, yet unhurt, except for his pride,
The man skulks away for a place to hide.
The crowd a-cheers, the duel now at an end,
They gather round him like a long lost friend.
Not all glory is won with blood and spit,
But some are won with just finesse and wit.
This is now the end of the yarn I spin
Of the scarlet lad, Rykolii Rufkyn.

Greg Kilberger

-THE PATH UNSEEN-

I rip the pages from my future
Unwilling to follow what has been written for me
I scan the entries in life's journal
For hints of which path is most hopeful and free
I dare not choose the left path
It is overgrown with tired words of the past
I can not follow the right path
For the dangers loom to strike as I pass
So I take up my pen, my chin in hand
And realize that I need not choose
Instead of a path set before me, I can
Author my own, and traverse it, win or lose.

-SYMPATHY FROM THE DEVIL-

Some call me Baalzebul
Others Beelzebub
I've even heard Mephistopheles
Ah, but there's the rub.

All the names and all the deeds
I've supposedly used and done
But why call me evil when
I'm only having fun?

Yes, sometimes, a woman must die
Or a man's crops turn black
Perhaps something more subtle
The proverbial dagger in your back?

But *my* fingerprints are not there
And yet I stand accused
So often, it seems, the name of Lucifer
Is maliciously abused.

I only live to gain your souls
Many of you say
In truth I feed upon your fears
They keep my hunger at bay.

Your blame, you see, is misaligned
Your condemnation is wrong
And if you learn of its true home
You'll find the journey not long.

So when you rise to challenge me
Don't be so sure, don't stand so tall
For when you view my true reflection
You'll see I live inside you all.

Greg Kilberger

-THROUGH THE AIR-

Through the air it flies
Spinning on its side
People feel they live and die
Upon its arching ride
It's hit and kicked
No respect for it at all
But everyone wants to
Own it, the game ball

-THE AUDITION-

I see them.
Sitting among the darkened seats,
Jotting down the fate of some other.
As I wait in the wings.
The scratching of pens, the shuffling of feet.
A muted cough, these surround me.
The scent of musty chairs mingles with fear.
As one drop of sweat races down my spine.
My adrenaline begins to rise.
My name echoes within the ebon chamber.
I know I am now free to become.
I have no fear, only the air, and the stage.

Greg Kilberger

-EYE-

I TOOK THE FIGURE
OF A DRAGON THAT MY GRANDMOTHER
MADE ME AND PUT IT ON THE TABLE. IN
THE DIM LIGHT I LOOKED INTO ITS EYES. WHEN
YOU LET YOURSELF UNFOCUS, YOU CAN SEE SO MUCH MORE.
THE EYES TOOK ON A DEPTH, A SENSE OF TRUTH. AS I STARED, I
FOUND I COULD SEE ALL OF WHAT WAS THIS DRAGON. HIS HUNGER AND
HIS WISDOM SHONE. THE PRIDE AND LOVE OF THIS GREAT WYRM GLEEMED
IN THOSE IMMENSE ORBS. THROUGH THE CENTURIES, ALL THE DESIRES,
FEARS, FEATS, AND FAILURES HE HAD EVER KNOWN. IN THAT
DIM ROOM OF MY HOUSE, I HAD LIVED FOREVER THROUGH
THOSE EYES, AND I WAS FILLED WITH WONDER.
SOMEONE SAID THE EYES ARE THE WINDOW
TO THE SOUL. I DISCOVERED THAT IN
THE EYES OF THAT DRAGON,
I COULD SEE MY
IMAGINATION.

-THE MORNING KILLS-

The ground outside the front door is covered in a false snow
As the ladies keep busy through gossip and plucks.
The sweet smell of fresh blood fills the air where I stand
Over by the pen with the living, not knowing their luck.
As another swift blow severs bone, and flesh
And the dead runs from me, as if to get away,
I close my eyes and think about the evening
When my dreary life turns from work to play.
Lively polka music dances about the room
Coming from an old dial radio on the counter.
While my sister sets the table up for six,
My brothers and I sit and engage in euchre.
When my old man finally comes in from the fields
Dirt under his fingers and grime on his face,
He greets us with a hearty hello, and heads to the bathroom,
Where he washes his hands and comes back to take his place
At the head of the table, with the rest of us kids
Just waiting for Mother to bring out the bird.
She opens the oven and we all catch the smell
Of butter-basted fresh kill, the best smell in the world.
With green beans and carrots, salad and fresh rolls.
The meal is complete and we all will have our fill,
Just another normal evening of food and music and fun
To counter all we've done and all the work left still.
So as the ladies pluck and I chop off another head
I think how lucky I am to be growing up here,
With love and food and family all around.
I vow next time I won't piss and moan and complain
When I'm getting bored or tired or down.

Greg Kilberger

-POETIC VERSE-

If I take the word *red* and rhyme it up with *bed*
Is that still poetry? Is that poetry bad?

If I say love is like a flower, it smells sweet for about an hour.
Is that painful to read? Does it make you mad?

What if I use flavorful verbiage, without meaning or message?
Is it still poetic verse or something worse, just sad?

-DRINK-

Sitting in this bar just waiting for you
Still a little early, so I'll have a drink or two
Swapping jokes with the 'tender, he seems nice
Sipping on a Rusty Nail chilled over ice
The music starts bumping, the crowd flows in
Might as well have some tonic and gin
One shot of tequila, an ice cold beer
We're sure to have fun when you get here
I guess you're running late but I'm feeling fine
Never knew chips went so well with this wine
Last call happens and here you are not
Oh, what the heck, bring me one more shot
My cab pulls up, time for me to go
But I'll be back tomorrow, maybe then you'll show

Greg Kilberger

-STRANGE-

I have always been organized
Strange
All my parts in their place
different
Lately my wisdom is not so wise
odd
My logic now is uneasy to trace
confused
So I look without for answers within
lost
To find the truth I know hides there
found
I must be willing to lose in order to win
danger
Whoever said that life was all fair?
Forever

-NOURISHMENT-

The rain nourishes the world.

It makes the plants grow and gives us the beautiful flowers of spring.

Without it we face drought and dust and hunger.

So why do so many people complain about the rain?

Getting wet won't hurt them, but you would think it was a traumatic experience.

I like the rain.

Walking in the rain is like no other journey.

It is a journey that nourishes the soul.

Greg Kilberger

-TEMPO-

There is only one problem with writing down these words.
You can't hear them.
See them, yes. Read them, yes.
But is how you read them how they are said?
Perhaps. perhaps I pause.
For contemplation, for complication.
Do you feel the pauses in the words, or do you just read?
I wish I knew that.
In a poem without meter, how do you gauge the tempo?
Say it out loud. Say it out loud.

-INCOMPLETE PICTURES-

Incomplete pictures too close to see all
Oddly shaped piles ready to fall
Piece them together both joy and strife
Parts of a puzzle these days of your life

Greg Kilberger

-LIZARDS-

Lizards.
Lizards are green.
Lizards eat a lot of food.
And lizards shit. They shit everywhere, they shit all over.
There's lizard shit all over the desert.
The desert is hot and sweaty.
And when you're in the desert you sweat and you can't breathe
so you sit down to catch your breath.
And when you sit, you sit in lizard shit.
It gets all over your pants, like Levi's or Guess jeans.
Really expensive jeans that you can only buy in expensive
stores.
Stores that don't and won't sell lizard shit.
You can go to K-Mart to get cheap, inexpensive jeans, but
their toy selection is quite limited.
So you go to a big toy store.
Like Toys-R-Us, where they sell everything, even G.I. Joe men,
and tanks, and jeans, and miniature deserts.
With plastic lizards on them.
But no toy store would dare sell lizard shit.
Besides, who would buy it? Would you? I hope not.
But G.I. Joe men, everyone buys.
Big ones, little ones, red ones, green ones.
Lizards are green, too.
But not all of them, some are brown, just like –
Lizards.

-IGUANA-

Waiting for the light.
It is still and so am I.
No movement, no activity, no desire.
I remain in this flux until the light.
Then the light and I must climb.
Reach a pinnacle to reach the light.
Let it's warmth revive my blood, give me energy.
Ah, warmth- now I eat, I drink, I survey my domain.
Try to stretch the perimeters.
But soon it will end, so I find my pinnacle and bask in the light.
I know I can store up enough to last through the night.
Take in all the light.
No movement.
No activity.
Just desire.

Greg Kilberger

-VACATION-

The sky
    With its streaks of white
The pool
    Reflecting the light
Bikini top
    Puts eyes in flight

Blue is alive this day

Vibrant
    Is how the trees appear
Quickly
    Lizards dart far and near
Timeless
    Is how each day is here

Wish I could always stay.

-TRUTH-

What do you do when you don't know
which way to look, which way to go
what do you do when you can't see
the proper path on which you should be
what do you say when you don't know
how to express or how you can show
what it is that you truly feel inside
when those words won't come to mind
take a deep breath and you will see
all you must do is speak truthfully.

Greg Kilberger

-PLEASURE AND PAIN-

```
PLEASURE
a   IF YOU LET ME TRY I CAN MAKE YOU SMILE
i   s   TAKE YOUR SHIVERING SKIN AND MAKE IT WARM
n       r   GIVE ME THE CHANCE AND I'LL GIVE YOU DESIRE
    t   y   r   AS THE WAVES OF PLEASURE CONSUME US BOTH
    h   i   a   s   WE WILL DWELL IN THE SATISFACTION AND GLORY
    i   n   b   s   e   AND YOU'LL SEE TOMORROW YOU WON'T FEEL THE PAIN
    s   g       h   l   n
                h   o   l   o
    a   t   e   l       t
    l   o   r   e   g   h
    l           o   o   e
        g   t   l       r
    y   e   a       a
    o   t   k   t   h
    u       e   h   e   n
            l   i   a   o
    c   n   h   n   d   t
    a   t   e   k       c
    n   o   r       s   h
                y   h   o
    t   h   y   o   e   n
    h   e   o   u   's
    i   r   u           y
    n       're  e   w   o
    k   p   e   n   h   u
        a       j   e   r
    o   n   n   o   r
    f   t   o   y   e   b
    ?   s               e
        ?   b   h   y   l
            e   e   o   t
            t   r   u
            t           o
            e   p   w   f
            r   a   a
                i   n   p
                n   t   l
                            e
                    h   a
                    e   s
                    r   u
                            r
                            e
```

-INTERNAL STRUGGLE-

This pressure builds down inside
With an urgency that you must abide
When it calls you must answer,
You know
You can't hold it back, just let it go
So take your place and feel release
And let this internal struggle cease

Greg Kilberger

-WORDS COME TO ME-

Words come to me as in a dream
Like frightened children they hide and scream
I try my best to set them free
Else they'll haunt for eternity
As I write them, they gain release
And their nighttime cries can cease

-ONE DRINK-

Just one drink to calm my nerves
    then I'll be fine. Then I will go on.
Just one drink to sip and relax
    I won't feel so edgy, won't feel so wrong.
One more drink, I've still got time,
    I'll have this one and then I'll go.
One more drink it will help me through,
    No one ever even needs to know.
One last drink before it's time,
    I need it to face what's coming next.
Or maybe I should just lie down,
    face it tomorrow, yes, that seems best.

Greg Kilberger

-NOTHING AT ALL-

Sometimes in my bed at night
I think I feel it crawl,
But when I open up my eyes-
Nothing,
Nothing I tell you, nothing at all.
The deep pitch of blackness surrounds me,
Screaming in my eyes-
I listen and grab for reality-
Where is it, who's is it-
And why won't it come when I cry?
Do you hear them,
Can't you feel them scratching from outside?
Don't succumb please, I beseech you.
Don't join me in this vacuum deep inside.
The words,
The words,
They are all drawn into the abyss
And they blind my mind's eye.

-CHANGE-

They say change is good.
I really do not know.
For change can leave you unsure
Of where it is you'll go.
Should I embrace change
for better or for worse?
It may be a blessing
or it may be a curse.
I am open to change,
for that is how we grow.
But change just for change's sake
is not the way to go.
Be open to new ideas,
experiences and such.
Take life as it comes
and don't fall out of touch.
Change can be scary,
Change can be slow,
But no matter the change you have,
There is one thing that I know.
Change is different.

Greg Kilberger

-NE'ER-DO-WELL-

Jack was a ne'er-do-well
Going through life without care
Every want was satisfied
His family had money to spare

Having no need for a job
He never cared to learn useful skills
He just reveled his days to excess
Pointless parties and random thrills

To himself, this was no concern
For Jack felt he was of good sort
But when asked to relay his many good deeds
He discovered he had none to report

For thirty-three years he thought only himself
In party and desires and drink
One day he considered all he had done
And decided to stop and to think

So at an outdoor café in Paris
(For that's where he was at the time)
He decided to find his direction
Instead of flowing through life without rhyme

But what could he do, he knew not of work
Just parties and women and such
And try as he might he could think of no job
That desired a self-centered lush

Seeing Life Along the Glass

As he sat pondering and sipping his drink
He noticed a lovely young lass
She was quite plainly dressed, yet carried herself
Such that Jack had to watch as she passed

The wind from the Seine whipped up that morn
Dashing the lady's hat from her head
It bounced once toward Jack, then reversed
And rolled out into traffic instead

Startled, the lass reached for her hat
But Jack was already on his feet
He was making a dash for the young miss
As she turned to step out on the street

He leapt for her wrist to stop her pursuit
But the girl thought Jack was just brash
Out onto the road she turned and she fled
And proceeded to cause such a crash

But Jack didn't relent, he held and he pulled
And tossed her off of the street
She landed hard, but he saw she was safe
Just as an auto and his legs happened to meet

Up in the air he flew like a doll
Arms flailing and legs flip and flop
With a screech and a scream all the street
Came to a heart-wrenching stop

The lass, suddenly aware of it all realized
How close she had been to death
Rushed to Jack's side, eyes full of fear
Hoping this wasn't his last breath

Greg Kilberger

Now Jack spends each day in this single chair
Doing whatever his fancies bid
But each day he thinks on that one Paris morn
When Jack the ne'er-do-well finally did

-DEMON-

Ebon claws, dripping hate,
Anger's own perpetual state.
Questing ever to destroy hope,
And leave it hanging from misery's rope.

It rises from darkness, born from fear,
The unknown demon is finally here.
It knows no love and feels no pain,
It thrives to rend and cut and maim.

At first it stalks only at night,
But soon grows bold, walks in the light.
It hungers to feast upon our flesh,
And drink deep from life's last breath.

Humanity feeds the beast's desires.
Without knowing, we fuel the fires.
With anger, deceit and lies,
We bring about our own demise.

Greg Kilberger

-IN PLACE-

It shines in the light like the whitest gold
Its gleam hints at my fortunes foretold
I see it and it makes me stop and smile
I reminisce and think of you for a while
Forever it will stay in its special place
Through it I feel your touch, see your face
It is a piece of you, my special friend
This ring that I wear on my left hand

-OPINION-

I know one man's trash can be another one's treasure
One man's pain is another's pleasure.
I understand how one's wrong can be another's right,
Or how my day can still be your night.
But how can you see this as such a tragedy-
While I know it is the remedy?
Is it perspective or am I defective?
You may ask where is my heart, but it's right here.
It is my mind that doesn't grasp your fear.
Clarity- stability- a joy to see,
Why can't you be what I hope you to be?
And what is it that you need that I just don't see?

-YOU-

Through you, I can be me by not being me
On you, I box myself in and set myself free
In you, I can whisper and shout right out loud
For you, I close my eyes and still reach the crowd
With you, I can jump high, and fly and soar
When your curtain calls, I long for my next encore
To you, I want to give my souls last breath
By you I see birth and living and death
In my life's journal I write your name on every page
I love you, my mistress, my world, the stage

-ASSAY-

A blank page faces me,
The door is open wide
There is every possibility
Just waiting for me inside
Will I write of the future,
Or tales long since passed?
Can I be student or teacher,
And can they forever last?
Shall it be truth or fiction
Or maybe something in between?
Will the words become an addiction
And flow from scene to scene?
So as I stare and ponder,
Just sit and consider and mull
I realize with great wonder
That my page is already full.

Greg Kilberger

-WAITING ROOM-

Sitting waiting nothing to do
Where is he, he is not here
They tell you to wait but never how long
Leaving me time to wonder
Why do people pay every day
For the privilege of waiting for them?

-CUTTING WIT-

A shortish man known for rapier wit strolls into the pub.
> Well met, I see thee are well fed and yet undelighted.

The patrons find hat in one hand, the other on his hilt.
> Before you stands but a humble minstrel hiding from the chill.

Bowing low, he sweeps the floor and deftly re-crowns his head.
As he saunters up to the rail, hails friend and not as one.
> Good cheer and good days, good folk, and for the price of a mead,
> I'll bear witness to danger and lucky success of Rykolii Rufkyn, 'tis I

Spirits soar high and mead doth run, and so with a draught
And a smile gaily on his lips, his bardic tongue relates,
'Til one dull lout denies his fame, a challenge is dropped within.
Our brave young man does not retrieve, he simply laughs and wits.
> Give heart, good man, 'tis no offense, I only aim to please.

But the oaf is too sour, he draws danger and comes a near.
So the scarlet lad, Rykolii, drops glass and goes to waist.
Rapier and stiletto fly, faster than the wisp,
An intricate dance of whirling blades, feared and admired.
The lout stares, mouth agape, finds himself unarmed.
Then a twinkle in Rykolii's eye, he sees a chance for fun.
Onto the oaf, with a flick of his wrist, now the bore finds
His pants wrapped round his stance, his belt upon Ryk's point.
> I dare say, Good Sir, you might slander someone with your own girth.

And so with the bore justly put, the onlookers a laugh.
No more treats dare ensue, so Rykolii orders another mead.
And friend and not gather close for a fresh bardic gale.

Greg Kilberger

-MOODY STROKES-

It cuts like a razor jagged and deep
With dark moody strokes sorrow can reap
Its pleasures from your pains of the flesh
As truth tears into you, hope finds its own death
When terror surrounds you free from its bond
It feasts upon you, from now til anon
You try to fight it, but your struggle's in vain
As uncertainly gorges upon your soul's very pain
Inky blackness expands, to engulf all you know
As the curtain goes up, now it's time for the show

-BILE BEASTS-

Dark creatures crawl around inside my head.
They leave thoughts in my brain that are foreign to me.
I should hunt them down, evict them for good,
but I can't seem to find enough energy.
So I let these ideas fester
contort and twist and grow
until they become bile beasts of insanity,
and the beasts begin to roam across the prairie of my mind
their thundering hooves leave my mind's eye blind,
and so I sit and wonder just what will become
of my love and life and joy.
I mustn't listen to their howls, but they keep calling to me.
Calling me out to play.
It is not a game I can win.

Greg Kilberger

-SIMPLE-

Plain and simple
Simple contemplation
Thoughts full of contempt
For the full-bosomed temptress
Who had used some tempting tricks
To free me of my hard-earned treats
Treating me as a simpleton
A plain and simple one
Who's been undone

-CERAMIC DRAGON-

In the dim light I look into it's eyes.
I know they're only glass, but if I let myself unfocus,
I can see so much more.
In the abstracted details, the eyes take on a depth.
Is it fair to call it truth?
Now the orbs are immense, and I can see a new reality.
His ageless wisdom, his pride, his wealth of power.
He gives these to me to examine,
As he looks into me.
And when we finish our silent exchange,
My eyes are filled with majesty and pleasure
A thousand years old,
And his are filled with wonder.

Greg Kilberger

-3 SIDES 2 EVERY STORY-

You see it every day.
Take the stairs or the elevator
-or the escalator.
Against capitol punishment or for it
-or in certain conditions.
Love it or leave it
-or leave it alone.
Recycle everything or not at all
-or just those things that are handy.
An amendment right versus gun control
-or control those with guns.
Left wing and right wing
-or middle of the road.
But then there's anti-abortion and pro-choice…
Does that leave me with pro-abortion?

-POET-

I am a poet.
I use words.
To create color.
To evoke emotion.
I give voice.
To unthinkable thoughts.
I tell truths.
Even if unwanted.
I explore.
I expound.
I am.
A poet.

Greg Kilberger

-COMPUTER BRAIN-

I wish my brain was like a computer
and all my memories could stay organized.
I could transfer thoughts lightning fast
and turn images into jpegs right from my eyes.
I could play music inside my head all day
or just whenever I got a little too bored
with playlists to highlight my particular mood
all neatly arranged and properly stored.
I would no longer forget someone's name
that I met that one time several weeks ago.
I could recall the whos and whats and wheres
I wouldn't need to guess, I would just know.
If my brain ran on quad core processors
and had more than enough RAM to spare,
I could recall every word you ever said
and every outfit you happened to wear.
You would be amazed at how I know it all
no one can remember every last detail.
but with my computer-like brain, each
conversation could be read like in an email.
But when you decide to give me pain
and cause lag where no files can be read,
I could just press down control-alt-delete
And reboot your ass right out of my head.

-UNFOCUSED-

Everything is abstract.
Indirect.
Recognition is reduced.
Navigation is hindered.
Colors become amalgams.
The world around becomes fuzzy.
And yet, sometimes
I seek out that view.
I will sit and stare at my world.
Unfocused, unclear.
Without glasses.
Sometimes,
That is when I see the most truth.

Greg Kilberger

-ALONG THE GLASS-

As you go through life's journey, you may find times
When the world is loud and you cannot hear your head.
You need to get away from it all, so you can find your truth.
Do not let it become too heavy, take a breath, take your time.

Put your paddle in the water.

Feel the breeze, drink it in, explore all you encounter.
And as you glide along that glass, I hope you find your way,
Whether you decide to circle the lake or head on downriver.

Seeing Life Along the Glass

Seeing Life Along the Glass

-HAIKU-

Tomorrow will come
Today's fears can lay and rest
To let new begin

Greg Kilberger

-TOMORROW'S YESTERDAY-

The Day after today
    Things may be clear
        Lose some of the fear
            How I wish I may
Know what will come
    When tomorrow is here
        Will we be as we are
            And not suddenly undone
Tomorrow's yesterday
    Is where I am now
        And although I know how
            I still cant find the way
Deep in my soul
    I know I know you
        And you know me too
            Together we are whole
And yet now apart
    I do not feel strong
        Yet I must carry on
            For the sake of my heart

-PSYCHO-

Cyan liquid flows within
Out of sight contained by skin
Bringing air and food and life
It's flow altered by a knife
Cutting shallow adds more time
To watch it drip and count the time
As the heart's rhythm hits its beat
Til this becomes a hunk of useless meat

Greg Kilberger

-INSIDE-

She loves me, but not as I am.
Confusion washes over her.
Fear rushes through me.
She wants to leave.
I will fight.
I will lose.
I will die.
Inside.

-LESSONS-

There is no pleasure
There is no joy
There is no pleasure
Without pain.
There is no sunshine
There is no clear sky
There is no sunshine
Without rain.
You cannot hide
You cannot run
You cannot hide
It will find you.
You should listen
You should learn
You should listen
It will be true.
I long for the rain
For it brings growth
I long for the rain
For what it will show.
I long for the pain
For it brings growth
I long for the pain
For what I will know.

Greg Kilberger

-MEMORIES-

Pit of my stomach
Pit of my soul
Feeding my hunger
Keeping me whole
Bile and humours
Balance my pain
Destroy my memories
Keeping me sane

-LOSS-

She's supposed to be dead, how can I still see her
In the park, on the street, in my mind.
I watched her let go of her hold on this life, yet
When I open my eyes, it is hers that I find.
Is this madness; is this sorrow, or a ghost I see?
What can be gained, past and present intertwined.
When I try to let go, she won't let me slumber
Her spirit beside me, so cruel and so kind.

Greg Kilberger

-WINTER-

The recent snowfall is a cold blanket for the ground. The trees, devoid of their shawl of leaves, grasps vainly at the wind as I walk along the lane, wrapped up in my memories. I see my chilling breath and hear the crunches beneath me, and yet numbness of the flesh is unaffected by the coat of sorrow cast about me, weighing down my shoulders and resting heavy upon my soul.

Sweet desire, longing joy, the loss of my Lena has taken them from me. I remember that winter, as if it was still chilling my bones, so cold. That first frost was a harbinger of the many shrouds to fall that year. The snow covering the earth, my heart's sorrow, the shroud of death. Woe to those who say life goes on. It does not. Pain pauses time. It allows you to dwell in your misery without release, without exit.

I look at old photographs, trying to bask in the glories of the spring, the sun, the warmth, the simple pleasures that Lena showed me. I remember, but do not relive. Happiness is a foreigner to me. Even watching videos of those days simply reminds me of what is lost. But there must be something for me for the future... some purpose. I seek guidance for freedom, a way out of this labyrinth of despondency.

I am still young, but my heart and my head feel enfeebled, exhausted. The drive of life withers within. More and more I choose to be numb, for when benumbed I no longer need to acknowledge my loss. Loss is pain, pain is life, life is but a disease we must all endure. When I open my eyes each day, it is unconscious, uncaring, unfeeling. Natural curiosity is replaced by apathy; the frost of death my only goal.

-WHAT TO DO-

What do you do
When you want something
But it is out of your grasp?
What do you do
When you love someone
But they think it won't last?
What should you do
When it is dark
And it's still supposed to be day?
What will you do
When your everything
Decides that they can't stay?
Do you fight?
Do you hide?
Do you curl up and cry?
Or do you take it
Like a man
And let them say goodbye?

Greg Kilberger

-MORBID THOUGHTS-

I have always had morbid thoughts.
Thoughts of destruction in my life.
What would I do if I got cancer.
How would I react to having a bad accident that left me without a limb.
What would I do if I went blind.
I have many times thought about those situations.
What would I do if one of my sons died.
Or my parents, or my wife.
They pop up in my head randomly, and I always ended up being strong in my mind.
Facing each calamity with resolve and stoic determination.
And yet, with all my morbid thoughts, I never considered how I would react if my wife decided that our love was over.
And that we were no longer to be.
And now that I am facing that crisis, I am not just accepting the situation and stubbornly carrying on.
Instead of gritting my teeth and accepting, I am crying and begging and pleading.
I feel sick all the time and cannot imagine life alone.
Of all the problems I faced in my mind, none were as bad as my reality.
Maybe that is why I never imagined it.
They say misery loves company, but I would be better off if misery stayed home and my dear love came back.

-2 MINDS-

I am of two minds about you.
The first tells me to stop fighting.
Your decision is made, your path set.
My resistance simply pushes you farther, faster.
The light says go while I scream stop.
I should just accept defeat.
Let you go.
The second tells me to struggle more.
Fight for you, keep you ever closer to my heart.
Hover and border you until you see
That you will never lose me.
Hold you tight.
I am of two minds about you.
And both of them are wrong.

Greg Kilberger

-DIG DOWN-

Wallowing in your own self-pity is like trying to dig yourself out of a hole by digging down.
It only gets yourself deeper and deeper, farther and farther away from the light.
You aren't doing yourself any good, but it is so hard to stop.
It seems like the only natural recourse.
Even if you know you should view things differently, gain a new outlook on life, it is an impossibility.
Any other option is futile.
You must continue digging until you find that breakthrough that allows you to dig in a different direction.
I am still digging down.
The dirt gets harder and harder, but I keep digging.
If only I could pile the dirt back up.
Fill in the hole.
But I have thrown the dirt too far to recover.
I am lost.
What other course do I have right now, but to dig down.

-FRUSTRATION-

Frustration is so frustrating.
It is infuriating.
When you can't get what you want.
Or can't reach what you need.
Or can't find your desire.
Frustration breeds a darkness.
That moment when your chest tightens.
And the only choice is shake or lash out.
Primal screams.
Smashing things.
Or stand there, seizuring.

Greg Kilberger

-HATE MY LIFE-

I hate my life.
I hate my life right now.
Without you.
I hate my life.
I hate my life right now.
Without you.
The days are dark.
And my soul is bare.
I see your face.
Almost everywhere.
I kiss your lips.
In all my dreams.
But when I'm awake.
Nothing's as it seems.
I can't have you.
Cause you've gone away.
There is no tomorrow.
And I hate today.
I hate my life.
I hate my life right now.
Without you.
I hate my life.
I hate my life right now.
Without you.

-ANYMORE-

I don't know why that you don't love me anymore.
I don't know why you don't want to hug me anymore.
I don't know how I'm gonna live in this house alone.
And I don't know why you need to be out on your own.
But I know I won't be the same once you walk out my door.
Why oh why, can't you just love me anymore.

I see your face, it's everywhere that I turn.
I smell your hair, it is a memory that has burned
Itself upon my brain so long that I just can't let it go.
I think of you and wonder why, oh why do you have to go.
I try to fight the pain inside, but I end up on the floor.
I don't know why that you don't love me anymore.

I've spent my life loving you all that I can.
Without you here, I'll only be but half a man.
And they say I will get over you, it'll just take some time.
But I don't want to be over you, I just want you to be mine.
So I'll live my days and sleep my nights and pray to God above
That you will see in me the man that you can love.

And if that day shall come to be, I will be set free
From this prison of loneliness that has captured me.
And I'll take your hand and hold you tight and make you see the truth
That you were made for loving me and I for loving you.
And I will not forget the things that I have learned.
Patience, love and respect, that is what you deserve.

Greg Kilberger

So if there is a chance for us, I hope you try it soon.
But I would wait a hundred years if I had to.
Just to have you in my arms and have you as my own.
And prove to you that you can be all you want in this home.
I know I have let you down, but if I get this chance
Maybe we can live our lives as one long slow dance.

All these things I have said, I know they are true.
But they are only true for me; I wish they are for you.
But there's a chance that I am wrong and you will stay away.
And I will be all alone up until my dying day.
I hope that you find happiness once you go out that door.
Even if that means that I won't see you anymore.

-THE DEED-

Somewhere a man picks up a knife
    And rests the point over his heart.
His mind replays his wretched life
    It grasps upon a place to start.

His past days filled with labor lost
    Toiling at some menial job.
All that time, but at how much cost?
    Nothing left, all leisures robbed.

Now his childhood blinks into sight
    But his eyes close tight from memories rough.
He always felt things were not right
    His father's hand more than his mother's touch.

His twisted fate even gave him love
    Only to have his joyousness dashed.
His sweet young thing, his turtledove
    Found her rest in a fiery crash.

Somewhere a man cradles a knife
    And feels the burning of his heart.
After seeing what is his wasted life
    Feels nothing worthy stands apart.

So push has finally come to shove
    And he knows, as inspirations flash,
He has, in this world, nothing left to prove
    All its treasures revealed as trash.

Greg Kilberger

As he contemplates his final fight
    Should it be slow or in a rush?
The day waxes into night
    And settles into a primal hush.

All these thoughts his mind have tossed
    A worthless pawn, a useless cog.
Now grim belief his life well lost
    While devils cheer and angels sob.

Somewhere a man thrusts a knife
    And greets the blade with his heart.
As scarlet drains out his life
    His lips, a smile, with his depart.

-WINDOWS-

They say poetry is the window to the soul.
But I wonder what that really means.
Do they think my words can reveal
What I really feel?
I can wax poetic about pain
And about love lost
But the words I write cannot explain
How much it really cost.
Is it fair to compare my love
To some fragile thing
When things can come and go
But my love is everlasting?
Do I want to express myself,
For empathy or for purgation?
Either way it helps my soul
Find it's way from oblivion.
My words are a window to my soul
I wonder how that is true.
For my windows are all painted black
When I am here without you.

Greg Kilberger

-ANTACIDS AND WHISKEY-

I look out the window of this old house
Trying to figure out what went wrong.
Was I just too loud, was I just too soft,
Or did I just come across too strong?
The life that lived inside these walls
Now has given up the ghost.
And I am left here with the memories
Of what I desired the most.
When I close my eyes I still see
Everything trapped in my head.
Antacids and whiskey help me to breathe
But they don't help me to bed.
The spots on the carpet and the painted walls
Miss that delicate touch.
And I sit at this window watching the birds
And missing you oh so much.

-AT NIGHT-

I lie awake in bed at night thinking how we went wrong.
With eyes closed or open, I just suffer until the dawn.
Though you lie here next to me, we are worlds apart.
As you slumber soundly, I wrestle with the dark.
When I say I love you, you won't return the words.
Because though you still care, the fire has been purged.
You know that we are over, and yet I disagree.
For life without you, in my mind, is an absurdity.
So now I'll try to prove that we can love again.
Fan the flames of passion so you remember when
Our apples were each other's eyes and you will see the truth.
That today is just a trial in our path to death from youth.
These ups and downs we'll overcome but first we have to try.
If I thought there was no hope, I'd shrivel, wilt, and die.
So I wait and pray and lie in bed wanting you to choose
To open your heart to me again and chase away the blues.
Until that time I can do no more than simply let you be.
I hold your hand when you're asleep
and pretend you still love me.

Greg Kilberger

-JOY-

I have felt joy.
When I see her eyes.
When I sense her touch.
When I hear her voice.
Joy is in the memory.
It is in the pictures.
It is hidden in my soul.
But it has been locked away.
The joy I have now is an old joy.
A joy of the past.
Of times gone by.
Of wishes, and hopes, and dreams.
But when I look forward,
I do not see joy.
I see regret.
I see pain.
I want to have joy.
But how can I have it without her?
She is my joy.
And that joy has walked away.

-SLEEP-

I know what I want
I know what I need
But I can't have it
You won't give it to me
I close up my eyes
To get you to here
But you will not come
And let me disappear
I try as I can
I try as I might
But I am still awake
You won't visit tonight
They say this is caused
By my broken heart
That's why I just sit
Alone here in the dark
But what I want now
Is one simple thing
To just be asleep
And fuck what the day brings

Greg Kilberger

-THINK ABOUT-

It is 3am and I am wide awake.
    all I can think about is you
I lie in the dark and wish it is light.
    all I can think about is you
My stomach is angry, my heart is a mess.
    all I can think about is you
Why wont you rescue me, then you will see.
    all I can think about is you
That if you save me I can save you.
    all I can think about is you
I do all I can to get through this night.
    all I can think about is you
I don't know what I will do tomorrow.
    all I can think about is you

-YOU AND ME-

I can't believe it's over
I can't believe it's true
That you feel nothing for me
While I keep loving you
You tell me you need time
To figure out your life
So now I give you space
And I lose a wife
I only want you happy
But now that I'm alone
Your happiness saddens me
In this empty home
So I guess I will keep waiting
And praying that you return
Even though you say our love
Has sorely crashed and burned
Perhaps one day I will accept it
Or at least I hope that you'll see
That you and me will always be
But *us* I'll miss for eternity.

Greg Kilberger

-EAT THE BULLET-

If you find yourself at the end of your rope,
do you cling to the frazzled ends,
do you let go,
or do you tie yourself a noose with that same rope?
If you are lost in the darkest of woods,
would you randomly roam around the trees,
pick a direction and walk,
or sit down,
resigned without hope?
When your soul is maimed by another,
do you hunt them down,
ready to unleash your revenge,
or do you simmer and boil,
only to lash out at some unsuspecting sot?
When my heart is broken,
and I cannot see any way to repair it,
do I cry like a baby,
do I flee like a wanted man,
or do I simply take a deep breath and eat the bullet?

-LIGHT AND DARK-

To write of life or speak of death
    The dark and light fights for space
    To cloud or brighten upon my face
And give me cheer or take my breath

The joy, it wants to feel my smile
    To savor all that is good and true
    In days, in nights, both old and new
To take the time to pause a while

The ebon side of my heart is grim
    Its blackest thoughts are sharp and rife
    There is no pleasure within this life
So turn the light from bright to dim

Greg Kilberger

-SHOTGUN POETRY-

My chest feels hollow, like an empty oil drum,
without your love to fill it.
My head is full of these thoughts of you
and I cannot ignore it.
I don't sleep, I don't eat, and I can't seem to smile
with you away from my life.
I try to move, but like a snail I go. Every step
is filled with strife.
My heart is a pit into which I will fall
and have no means of egress.
And there I will sit and fester and rot
until I am aught but a mess.
The day you left is the day that we died
and now I want to join us.
You have chosen to live your life alone
no option for me, and thus
I shall make my way for as long as I can,
how long I cannot foresee.
Until I finally reach my end, and recite my
shotgun poetry.

-BLAME-

This is not my fault, this is because of you.
But I will take the blame if you ask me to.

To everyone else, I can be the bad guy.
But both of us will know the real reason why.

I love you and you know that is true.
But that doesn't mean I can't be mad at you.

If I let myself really express what I feel,
The anger I have hidden will become real.

I want to rail at the walls and break the doors,
Scream go to hell or something even more.

I want you to hurt as much as I do now.
Make you feel regret, that is what I avow.

But even if I knew how to hurt you deep,
I doubt I could allow you to feel like me.

So I will just stand here and take the blame,
And smile and pretend it's all the same.

Greg Kilberger

-LED-

Led. The act of having followed.
Lead. The bullet that you eat.
I wish you had led me to the light,
So I didn't need that lead tonight.
I would gladly give you my heart
Or my whole body limp at your feet.

-MEMORIES-

Torn asunder are the pages of my life.
I feel an emptiness deep inside.

I want to make the pain just disappear.
But I cannot when you are near.

And the problem is heaped double fold
when I hurt from memories old.

No matter where I look or where I go,
Visions of you is all that show.

In this song, in that dish, on that chair,
I see your face or smell your hair.

The pain will fade, that's what they say,
but I don't see that truth today.

I try to just ignore these open wounds,
but the bleeding won't stop soon.

So I breathe deep and open my eyes
and hope my heart will survive.

I hear it's darkest before the dawn.
It's black here, sun, so come on.

Bring me that light of a new day,
so I can forget my yesterday.

Greg Kilberger

-THE LAME DUCK HUSBAND-

I am a lame duck husband.
I am still married, but only in name.
My wife is still here, but only in one sense.
She no longer loves me.
Her soul is lost to me.
Seeing her every day is tearing me apart.
And there is nothing I can do.
I am a lame duck husband.
Eventually she will tell me it is time.
She will leave me.
I will be alone.
What use is getting mad?
It will not change things.
What use is getting upset?
It only causes me more pain.
I am a lame duck husband.
One day she will leave my home.
She will leave my life.
And I will love her still.
I will always love her.
We were one story being told together.
But now we are two stories.
Her story will be fresh and new.
And my story will be old and unread.
It is a story of lost love.
She lost her love, and I have lost her.
I am a lame duck husband.

-SHELL-

Black tears in the well
Rising up from my hell
Darkness is my only light
Touch is my only sight
Losing focus it almost helps
Trapped inside a broken shell

Greg Kilberger

-THE KEY-

Wait until you see what I have inside.
I have a secret that you will want to know.
All of my hints just make you wonder.
Until you finally ask me to show.

I think it is best to keep it for me.
If I give it to you, I will lose even more.
But you ask and I cannot resist what you are
So I give you the key that will open the door.

I wonder if you will even care to see,
Or simply just take it and throw it away.
I pray you can feel how much I care
For you, ever increasing by every new day.

But if it turns out that is not enough
With sullen resign I will distain,
And wander out into the fog of my life
Remembering the love and the pain.

-DARK DAY-

I have been living my life in a shell.
Hidden from the reality that has grown up around me.
She tells me that the love is dead.
She sees me as just another brick holding her in.
But I want her to be happy.
Do I let myself be broken to fix Her.
I don't know which way to fight.
Fight for me, fight for Her.
Can I find the path that is both?
Can I go down my own path?
Yes.
But I don't want to.
It is a path without Her.
For eighteen years all I have seen is the path with Her.
My feet are cold,
My head swims.
I know what I want.
I want to take Her in my arms.
Hold Her.
Hold Her until this all goes away.
But I fear
    That
        Will
           Not
              Work.

Greg Kilberger

-ICE CUBE-

There was a time when I thought I could have it all,
All the glories that life had to offer.
But I was young and foolish.
I was not aware yet that life is never ever after.
But now, I am much older and wiser.
I have learned through the trials of life.
And what I have learned is something I wish I had not known.
Happiness is fleeting, joy is temporary.
You can chase it, you can find it, but you cannot keep it.
Joy is an ice cube.
The harder you hold onto it, the faster it goes away.

-BUTTERFLY HEART-

I try to walk away, but I cannot seem to let me.
Even though I know that there is no other choice.
Instead of hope, now only anger wants to find me.
And I am afraid to let it finally reach my voice.

How can I go on alone when I don't want to be free?
But nothing I do or say can make you remain.
Like love's prisoner, you have captured me.
When you break these chains I will never be the same.

My mind says to be strong and simply carry on,
And eventually I will once again find happiness.
My heart says never forget, forgetting would be wrong,
And stuck here between these thoughts I am just a mess.

My butterfly heart feels like it is pinned onto a board.
Slowly it is beating out its last attempts at life.
My ship drifts away from where is was tightly moored,
As I cling to the rails and try to endure this strife.

The salty spray covers my face and soaks me through.
My knuckles are sickly pale from holding on too tight.
I just want to jump overboard and swim back to you.
But I don't know which way to go; it's too dark this night.

Greg Kilberger

-RADIO-

As I drive down the road with the sun up above
I see nothing before me 'cept our crumbling love
I drive and I wonder what I did wrong
That's when I notice that every new song

Is all about you, they are all about me
Of my loss, of your desire to be free
How can these songs that I have heard before
Suddenly open up so many new doors

Of my emotions, my love, and of my fears
I can't put them aside, I will just have to steer
My mind away from where it now dwells
I head down the road, only time will tell

How this journey of ours will end
I hear a new song past every bend
In the road, but still I can only drive on
Hoping to write the new "our song"

I know not where to go, I know not what to do
I know naught of my life, I only know you
Have come to a road where you have to choose
Which life to take and which one to lose

I just keep driving down this highway of mine
Wishing I would have noticed the signs
I wonder if I can put us back in place
As I feel the salt slowly run down my face.

-SHIP-

My marriage is a ship on the ocean of life
traveling along from shore to shore.
We plotted the course, myself and my wife
and set out for adventure by the score.

For years we sailed together through that sea
whether the winds were chilly or warm,
And even when the waves were rough on me
together we weathered out the storm.

Sometimes our journey would get off track
but never did we run our hull aground
We would find new ways to find our way back
and share the new treasures we found.

The sun and the air and the birds in the sky
made a world I would never defer
And even when the rains threatened to cry
I had no worries when I was with her.

But then she started to spend most her days
alone in the dark in the hold
I assumed that it was some type of phase
and she would come out of the cold.

I did not know she was in her own storm
one that I had helped to create
As she watched the swells continued to form
I did not know that it was too late.

But one day I heard a very loud splash
and I thought she had slipped overboard
Panicked, to the rail I had dashed
but could not see the one I adored.

Throwing a safety line was my only hope
so I ran to grab some that day.
As I stood on the deck throwing out ropes
I did not know she was swimming away.

Seeing Life Along the Glass

-WELL-

Someday you may find yourself at the bottom of a well.
Dark and wet and all alone with no easy way out.

You may feel trapped, you may feel abandoned,
And you have three choices from which to choose.

You can decide there is no way out, no escape.
And with that you will wait in the darkness forever.

You can hope someone comes along looking,
Finds you and throws you down a rope.

It is the easiest way out, but it also holds much danger.
Because if you wait too long for rescue, hope can change into despair,

And the well will only get deeper and deeper for you.
And if help does arrive, you may not have the strength to hold the rope,

And your safety line will only slip though your fingers.
Or you can decide to climb. Stick your fingers deep in the cracks.

Pull yourself up inch by inch. Though it causes sweat and blood.
You can climb out, no matter how deep. But you must try.

You cannot give up, you cannot falter. You must hang on.
And when you reach the top, it will be warm and sweet.

I am in the well, but I have decided to climb.
My nails are cracked and covered with blood.

Greg Kilberger

Sweat blinds my eyes. I am hungry and cold.
But I will fight to once again see the light.

The well is deep, but it is not the end, unless you let it be so.
Come with me. Let us climb.

Seeing Life Along the Glass

ABOUT THE AUTHOR

Greg Kilberger has a degree in both Theatre and English. As he likes to say, that way he can act like a writer. He lives in Iowa City, where he does what he can to pay the bills and keep food in the fridge. Currently, Greg considers himself a professional actor, writer, and poet. He intends to add to that professional playwright and novelist. He is old enough to know better, but thankfully young enough still to not care.

www.ingramcontent.com/pod-product-compliance
Lightning Source LLC
Chambersburg PA
CBHW071520040426
42444CB00008B/1737